Caution: Contents Under Pressure

Learning How to Handle Anger

Fran & Jill Sciacca

World Wide Publications
Minneapolis, Minnesota 55403

The **Lifelines** *Leader's Guide* is a publication free to all who request it. Write to: Lifelines, World Wide Publications, 1303 Hennepin Ave., Minneapolis, MN 55403.

Caution: Contents Under Pressure

World Wide Publications is the publishing ministry of the Billy Graham Evangelistic Association.

Unless otherwise indicated, Scripture quotations are taken from The Holy Bible, New International Version. Copyright © 1973, 1978, 1984 International Bible Society. Used by permission of Zondervan Bible Publishers.

Scripture quotations marked TLB are taken from The Living Bible, © 1971 Tyndale House Publishers. Used by permission.

ISBN: 0-89066-199-5

Printed in the United States of America

Why "Lifelines"?

Who in the world are Fran and Jill . . . is it Sky-Ocka??

The name "Sciacca" (actually pronounced "Shock-a") is probably not a familiar name to you. Let me take you on a quick trek through our lives, so you will know who we are and why we care so much about you.

Fran grew up in the shadow of older identical twin brothers who were football stars. While their photos and accomplishments appeared regularly in newspapers and magazines, Fran found himself wondering who he was besides "the twins' little brother." In high school, he decided to take his talents "elsewhere," completely out of the arena of athletics — he set out to become the best bass guitarist he could be. His rock band was a success, and soon Fran also made it to the pages of the newspaper. On one occasion, he played in front of five thousand people at a "battle of the bands" in Milwaukee, Wisconsin. Fame became Fran's total focus in his search for identity. He was popular at school and was elected class president for three years.

In college, Fran quickly blazed his way to the top of his fraternity. The professional status of his new rock group also gave him personal pride. The band's popularity soared beyond the college campus, and Fran began doing "warm-up" for nationally known entertainers such as Chase and B. J. Thomas. He had finally "arrived" — or so he thought. But why, he wondered, was the feeling of emptiness still lodged so deep in his soul?

Then in one year's time, the band began to break up, his girlfriend dumped him, and he received the devastating news that one of his brothers had been seriously wounded in the Vietnam War. It was as if someone had let the air out of his world. He felt alone in the universe. Even his twelve years of religious education in a private school didn't help him.

About this time, God brought a friend into Fran's life who had just committed his own life to Jesus Christ. Late one night in a quiet dorm room, Fran heard from him about the depth of God's love. For the first time, Fran had reason to believe that he was a valuable person, not because he was "cool," or a popular bass guitarist but because the God of the universe loved him and had paid the penalty for his sin. Fran found the identity he had always longed for in the person of Jesus Christ.

Jill's Journey

I grew up in "the suburbs," graduating with a class of more than seven hundred students. My years in high school could best be characterized by my quest to know, "Where's the party?" But when I was alone, I often thought about life and death — even suicide. I wrote poetry that exposed my inner fears, but felt they were "safe" as simple assignments for English class. As best I could, I squelched my spiritual emptiness by dancing, partying, working a little, and playing a lot.

My folly and flippant approach to study in high school forced me to be on probation for the first quarter of college. I buckled down to get good grades, but somehow managed to maintain my carefree lifestyle "to the max." I was dating a gifted art student, and together with other friends we embraced the sixties counterculture. Our philosophy boasted that peace was possible; we could affect society and bring about lasting change. We were the answer to all of America's problems.

Yet, in two years' time, I witnessed the tragic folly of the sixties philosophy in vivid detail. A best friend from high school had burned out on drugs. Another had died while on drugs. I had seen that our protests against the Vietnam War were leading to prison sentences. People were losing heart, dropping out. My boyfriend had been committed to a psychiatric ward in a hospital. My best girlfriend, who had entered college on a scholarship, had quit, disillusioned with life. My rock-star heros had fallen from the thrones I'd placed them on. Jimi Hendrix had died. (I had been in the front rows at one of his concerts.) Jim Morrison was gone. Drugs and death seemed to go together. We were not the answer to America's woes — we were part of the problem!

So I fled from the fast lane and started studying philosophy, searching for answers but finding none. Finally, I desperately cried out to the God I had learned about in Sunday school as a child. I had always believed in him, but never realized that I could know him personally. Committing my life to him, I made him my Lord and found the peace I hadn't found in all my searching. I joined the ranks of the revival on our college campus, the one that had also swept Fran into the faith. We were radical, but now we had an anchor and a purpose that really was destined to succeed.

And Then, Fran & Jill

We were married after graduation from college. Our first home was in Wisconsin, out in the country, where we attended a small church. There we immediately gravitated to the youth. Three years and one son later, the Lord led us to Denver, Colorado, where Fran went to seminary. While in Denver, we were again drawn to teens as Fran did field work at a local church. Two years and another son later, the Lord led us to Colorado Springs Christian School, where Fran taught high-school Bible for several years. Now we also have the blessed bonus of twin daughters.

We needed to tell you all this for two reasons: First, everything that these studies deal with comes out of our own experience. Second, in many of the things that you're going to look at in *Lifelines: Getting a Hold on Life,* we totally "blew it." So not only do we understand the issues at hand, we also know the pain and temptation that go with the territory.

We believe that a genuine relationship with Jesus Christ and with those who are committed to him is the most fulfilling and exciting thing on this sometimes perplexing planet! We're not talking about people who "play church." We're talking about those who are really serious about falling in love with, and following, the One who died for us.

So be assured that your struggles are familiar to us. They are foes that we have fought too. They are battles that we often lost. But we know there is a way of victory, and we want to help you discover that door of hope.

We pray that, through a personal study of God's Word, you will gain a new vision for a meaningful life, walking with the Lord and living in victory.

Fran and I are a fun team. He is the architect; I am the builder. You will find the Bible study section of each chapter designed by Fran. I have helped Fran put a personal touch to the studies by telling a story you can relate to, about someone who has been a part of our lives. (Names, gender, and nonessential details have been altered to protect the privacy of those involved.)

There is one more thing we want you to know as you begin this Bible study — we really care about you!

What Is "Lifelines"?

Life is tough! Being a teenager is even tougher. You bounce somewhere between adulthood and childhood, ping-ponging back and forth, not really landing on either side, never really knowing which side you're supposed to be on at any given moment. The temptation to give in or give up may seem greater than you can bear. You probably feel as if you're sinking in a sea of pressures and problems too deep and wide to navigate. Let's face it, life's a battle. But . . . on the other hand, is that so unusual?

What does it take to make the first-string soccer team? What's the cost of working your way to first-chair trumpet in the school band? How long did you have to practice to become the best guitarist at school? Remember those early morning practices for the spring play? It seems as if everything significant has a price tag. Maybe that's the way it's supposed to be; maybe that's the way God planned it. But he also provides the help we need along the way. *Lifelines: Getting a Hold on Life* is one of those helpers.

"Lifelines" Is Different.

Lifelines: Getting a Hold on Life is different. It won't help you "sail" through life, because nobody sails through life. But *Lifelines* will be honest with you about life, about God, about yourself, about your choices and your dreams. *Lifelines* promises to "put the cookies on the bottom shelf," to meet you right where you are and deal with the things that you have to deal with each day. It promises to provide answers where there are answers, and to ask questions where they need to be asked.

But, just as in the rest of life, there are some costs that go with these Bible studies. What are they? Simply this: *Lifelines: Getting a Hold on Life* promises to be honest with you, but you've got to be honest with yourself. And even more important — you've got to be honest with God. These studies are built on the presupposition that the Bible is God's Word. That means that your opinions and feelings have a genuine place in your life, but the final place is reserved for God's Word.

This Bible study cannot change your life; only God can do

that. But, God can't guide a parked car. You're the one who's got to cooperate with God as you carefully work through this study. You've got to be willing to let the Lord into your life, into your problems and pressures, into your battle. He wants to be beside you whether you are defeated or determined. If you are willing to pay this price, *Lifelines: Getting a Hold on Life* could very well be one of the most exciting things that happens to you this year.

Things to Keep in Mind:

Here are some important thoughts to keep in mind as you begin:

1. God is not a coach. He doesn't have a checklist for your performance. He loves you. In fact, he loves you just as you are as you begin this study.

2. Apply what you learn to yourself. Resist the urge to think of others who "really need to hear" what you are learning.

3. Be faithful. Whatever your commitment is, whether to a group or simply to yourself, keep it. Make it your goal to finish the study.

4. Be realistic. Weeds grow quickly, but an oak tree takes time. Look for small ways to grow. If you set goals that are too tough, you'll become discouraged. Small victories will encourage you to keep going.

Lifelines: Getting a Hold on Life accepts the fact that much of life is a battle for you. God wants you to win the battle. But remember: You can't have a victory where there's been no fight. You may fall — we all do — but learn to stand!

How to Use This Bible Study

This Bible study is part of a series entitled *Lifelines: Getting a Hold on Life*. Each study in the series centers around a single issue that you as a teenager face in the twentieth century. This study, *Caution: Contents Under Pressure,* is one of four that deal with the subject of emotions.

The theme of *Caution: Contents Under Pressure* is anger. It seems like the whole world is ticked-off sometimes! The check-out lines of grocery stores, the streets and highways, and above all, the hallways of our schools seethe and pulse with angry people. In *Caution: Contents Under Pressure,* you'll see that anger is one of man's oldest emotions. You'll examine the difference between healthy and unhealthy anger and find answers to question like these:

> *Is anger always a sin?
> *What happens if I refuse to admit and deal with my anger?
> *How *do* I deal with my anger?
> *What makes *God* angry?

Each chapter of this study includes a real-life story, some personal study questions, and a summary discussion. Look for one major truth, a "Lifeline," as you go through each chapter. If there are specific things the study asks you to do, be sure to do them. The insights you pull out of these pages won't help you until you begin to put them into practice.

The only things you will need to complete this study are a Bible, a pen, and an open heart. We suggest that you use a version of the Bible that is easy to read, such as the *New International Version or The Living Bible*. Make sure that your Bible has both the Old and New Testaments. You may also want to have a spiral notebook to record thoughts and ideas that come to you while you study.

If you study *Caution: Contents Under Pressure* in a group, you may find the optional group discussion questions in "The Bottom Line" section at the end of each chapter helpful.

There is another optional section near the end of each chapter entitled, "His Lines." These are a few verses from the

Bible that might be helpful as you seek to make the "Lifeline" from that particular chapter a reality in your own life. You can memorize these verses, put them on your mirror, in your locker at school, or on the dashboard of your car. Plant them anywhere they can prompt you to remember the truth when you need it the most.

If you find *Caution: Contents Under Pressure* encouraging, you may want to study one of the other three books in the *Lifelines: Getting a Hold on Life* series on emotions:

Kick the Fear Habit
Putting Fear in Its Place

Does Anyone Else Feel This Way?
Conquering Loneliness, Depression,
and Thoughts of Suicide

Is This the Real Thing?
What Love Is and What It Isn't

Still more *Lifelines* books are listed on the back cover of this book. The "Introductory Series" is designed especially to present the gospel message. Please consider sharing them with your friends!

1

Who Lit Your Fuse?

Opening Lines

Being the firstborn in a family has its drawbacks. The role means more responsibility, more work, more rules, and usually more disciplinary action! Firstborn status also requires participation in an awkward experiment known as *parenting*. Mom and Dad are generally just starting to get things all scoped out by the time the second or third child comes along.

The eldest in the family, however, has a personal agenda all his own. There is an assumed God-ordained right to boss, badger, and bully the younger brothers and sisters, especially when Mom and Dad aren't watching! Fights among brothers and sisters aren't anything new. In fact, there isn't a person alive who has had a brother or sister who can't recall feelings of intense anger that welled up within them — feelings that desperately sought an avenue of release. Anger goes back . . . well, just how far *does* it go back?

Adam and Eve were the original "first couple." Obviously, this also qualified them for the honor of being the first parents.

Their first adventure in parenting, however, came to a tragic end. They discovered the body of their younger son, Abel. Their firstborn, Cain, was also missing. Adam and Eve were well aware of the constant arguing and bickering between their sons. And you don't have to be Sherlock Holmes to reconstruct what happened that day. If you had two sons who happened to be the only two children living at that point in history, and one was murdered and the other was missing . . . well, the conclusion would be pretty clear.

What could have brought about Abel's death? More so, what connection, if any, does that day in a Middle Eastern field have to do with *you* almost eighty centuries later?

On the Lines

The first time *anything* appears in the Bible is always significant. For example, in *Kick the Fear Habit* we saw that the first emotion Adam and Eve experienced *toward God* after their first sin was fear.

In this chapter we'll look at the first recorded emotion expressed, after mankind's fall, by one human being to another. It's found in the story of Cain and Abel, in Genesis 4.

1. Looking at Genesis 4:1-2, do you think Cain and Abel were alike or different? Explain.

_____

_____

2. Read Genesis 4:3-5. Does God's treatment of Cain seem "fair" to you? ☐ yes   ☐ no   Explain.

_____

_____

What was Cain's emotional response to what God did?

_____

_____

3. Toward whom was Cain angry? (Think hard, look closely!)

_____

4. Look at Genesis 4:6-7. Here is God's response to Cain's anger. God asks Cain three questions, then makes one statement. Write them out below:

QUESTION A: _____

QUESTION B: _____

QUESTION C: _____

STATEMENT: _____

5. Look at what you wrote for question C above. Now, compare it to your answer to the first part of question 2 of "On the Lines." Did you accuse God of being "unfair" to Cain? Does what God said to Cain in question C shed some new insight on what must have happened that day? If so, what?

_____

_____

6. From Genesis 4:7, do you think Cain had already sinned by being angry, or that his anger could *lead* him to sin? Explain, using God's question and then his statement from this verse.

_____

_____

_____

Use your answer above to explain what happened in Genesis 4:8.

_____

_____

7. So, anger appears in the Bible as the first documented emotion man expressed toward another human being. In summary, write out your personal answers to the following three questions:

(1) Is anger (in and of itself) good or bad?

_____

(2) Toward whom is anger ultimately directed?

_____

(3) Toward whom is anger normally expressed?

_____

Between the Lines

1. What are (or were) your current thoughts about anger? Check the ones below that represent your thoughts or feelings.

- ☐ anger is always bad
- ☐ only weak people become angry
- ☐ anger is always a sin
- ☐ angry people always show it
- ☐ anger is totally controllable
- ☐ anger is always destructive
- ☐ keeping quiet is a sign of controlling anger
- ☐ expressing anger is always healthy

2. Take the short quiz below.

ACTIVE ANGER

1. Do you frequently raise your voice or hit things?
     ☐ yes   ☐ no

3. Do you find yourself often engaged in arguments with others?
     ☐ yes   ☐ no

PASSIVE ANGER

2. In a disagreement, do you frequently refuse to speak even when others demand it?
     ☐ yes   ☐ no

4. Do you find yourself often engaged in mental arguments with others?
     ☐ yes   ☐ no

5. As a rule, do you show disrespect for authority?
□ yes   □ no

6. Do you frequently find yourself "bad-mouthing" authority figures silently, to yourself?
□ yes   □ no

7. Do you lose your temper more than most of your friends?
□ yes   □ no

8. Do you spend periods of time alone, especially when others want to be with you?
□ yes   □ no

9. Do you often find yourself being sarcastic and mean to people who mean a lot to you?
□ yes   □ no

10. Are your grades lower than they should be because of the way you are thinking or feeling?
□ yes   □ no

11. Do you find yourself using words like "hate" and "die" frequently (even jokingly)?
□ yes   □ no

12. Do you enjoy it when people (especially parents) can't get you to do what they want?
□ yes   □ no

13. Does the music you listen to or the musicians who play it advocate violence?
□ yes   □ no

14. Do you listen to music (alone) that advocates violence?
□ yes   □ no

TOTALS: yes ____   no ____

TOTALS: yes ____   no ____

Not everyone who is an angry person shows it. Did you know that? In fact, all the questions in the column on the right were designed to discover "passive anger," anger that does not usually express itself openly. However, though this anger is not destructive openly, it is very harmful to the individual who possesses it (loss of health, life, self-esteem, friends, and many other liabilities).

If you scored four or more "yes" answers in either column, there is a likelihood that anger plays a more significant role in your life than it should. If so, take a moment right now and spend five to ten minutes talking to God about it. Tell him what you've discovered and what you want to change. Also, ask the Lord to make the next five chapters of this Bible study especially personal, practical, and powerful.

Anger can be harnessed and useful. It can also be destructive and deadly. For now, let's simply seek to follow the clear teaching of this Bible verse:

> Dear brothers, don't ever forget that it is best to listen much,
> speak little, and not become angry (James 1:19, TLB).

In this verse, two things have to happen *first* in controlling anger:

(1)   I must be serious about "listening much" (trying to genuinely listen to what others are telling me rather than thinking ahead how to defend myself).

(2)   I must "speak little." Most of the problems that are created by anger are a result of what we *say*. Keeping your mouth shut can help minimize the problems anger produces even though it doesn't always deal with what brought on the anger.

Get a few three-by-five cards and write out (or draw, if you want to be creative) something to remind you of this principle from James 1:9. Let the words *much* and *little* trigger your memory to listen much and speak little.

Closing Lines

Genesis 4 is a sad chapter. It begins with the birth of Adam and Eve's two sons and closes with a chilling murder and the banishment of Cain. This story records the first acting out of sinful anger in the Bible. It also clearly portrays the power of that emotion.

We also see from this story that anger is a part of mankind's sinful nature — every man and woman who has ever lived! It wasn't present in the Garden *before* Adam and Eve committed that first sin. But it showed up shortly thereafter.

It is also clear that Cain's anger was actually against God. He believed that God had shortchanged him and that God had been unfair. Yet, as can be typical of anger towards God, Cain vented his hostility against his own brother. Anger often *does* manifest itself towards others.

God did not punish Cain for *being* angry but for what he *did* with his anger. All anger is not a sin. Yet, God clearly warned Cain that his anger could someday get the best of him. And it did!

Cain stands as an everlasting testimony that anger is universal because sin is universal. But he also represents the absolute truth that *choices* are always involved in anger. The question is not *will* we become angry, but rather where did this anger come from and what will I do with it?

Cain blew it off, big time . . . but you don't have to.

Lifeline

Anger is a natural part of me; but it doesn't need to *control* me.

His Lines

James 1:19

Genesis 4:6-7

The Bottom Line
(For Group or One-on-one Discussion)

1. Discuss anger towards God. Does anyone feel angry at God because of a death, divorce, or failure of any kind? How can you handle this anger so that it doesn't master you?

2. Many law enforcement officials have made a link between some heavy metal music and violent or aggressive behavior. Do you think there is a valid connection between the two? Explain.

3. Why do you think people who profess to be unbelievers get angry at God when facing death or disasters such as war, earthquakes, floods, etc?

4. Do you see a connection between what this chapter discussed in reference to Cain, and the current rise of violent neo-Nazi groups such as the Skinheads? Explain.

2

Caution: Contents Under Pressure

Opening Lines

The door into my classroom didn't open that day — it detonated! Stephen's entrance followed the explosion; he was enraged. He was breathing like a bull about to meet the matador, exhaling huge bursts of air. He glared at me, his powerful shoulders tensed. He appeared ready to dismantle anyone who dared confront him. I actually wondered if today was the day I would die.

This wasn't Stephen's first grand entrance, and he had never actually laid a hand on me. In fact, I was one of the few friends he had left. But he also seemed like the type who might go berserk in a school, shooting anything that moved.

Stephen was an angry young man. It was the one emotion that had a real hold on his life. In his angry moments he had threatened teachers, fought with classmates, berated his frail mother, and totaled two cars. Anger for Stephen was not a passing emotion — it was a lifestyle!

He sat through my class that day, his body frozen in rage, his eyes fixed on an obscure spot on the carpet. The hour passed, I ended the lesson and dismissed the class. Stephen stayed, as I feared he would, waiting for me to notice his discomfort. Aware that the next move was mine, I said, "You don't seem like a happy camper today, Stephen. What's up?" Confident that this light comment would be like lancing a boil, I stood back. He then jumped up, arms waving, and paced the floor like a caged tiger. He began to spill out his latest tale of female injustice. Stephen went through girlfriends like a bee buzzing through a flower bed. Every relationship predictably ended with a conflict, followed by a tirade from Stephen. I was used to what was going on today because I'd been through it with him three or four times already that year.

After Stephen's anger began to lose some momentum, I asked if he'd like to take a walk outside with me. He knew it was my teacher's prep period and agreed. We headed for the door.

What could cause someone like Stephen to be so totally ruled by a feeling? There's obviously such a thing as *wrong* anger, but where does it come from, and is it a sin?

On the Lines

1. First, let's look at some examples of wrong anger in the Bible and see what we can learn from them. Below are four stories in which wrong anger is displayed. In the spaces provided, write out who was angry and why you think they were:

PASSAGE	WHO WAS ANGRY?	WHY?
Genesis 4:2-8	_____	_____
		_____
		_____
1 Samuel 18:5-9	_____	_____
		_____
		_____

2 Chronicles 16:7-10 _____   _____

_____

_____

Esther 3:1-6   _____   _____

_____

_____

Looking back at the four examples above, select one phrase from the short list below that best captures the probable cause of *all* these instances of anger:

☐ feeling used

☐ feeling a loss of power, control, or authority

☐ feeling unnecessary

2. Now let's do a short study of what the Bible has to say about wrong (inappropriate, sinful) anger. Look up the verses on the left and match them with the statements on the right.

_____ Colossians 3:8   A. I usually regret the things I do when I'm angry.

_____ Psalm 37:8   B. Controlling my anger is a sign of real strength.

_____ Proverbs 14:17   C. Anger can be responsible for cruelty.

_____ Proverbs 16:32   D. If I don't control my anger, it can result in something evil.

_____ Proverbs 27:4   E. Anger is a way of life for a fool (i.e., someone without wisdom).

_____ Ecclesiastes 7:9   F. Anger is one of the things God wants *out* of my life.

3. Read James 1:19-20 (especially verse 20). These verses reveal how serious wrong anger can be. Write out in your own words what verse 20 is saying, and why it is important:

WHAT IT IS SAYING

_____

_____

WHY IT IS IMPORTANT (see also 1 Peter 2:21-23)

_____

_____

_____

4. Summarize what you've learned from this chapter so far about wrong anger.

_____

_____

_____

_____

Between the Lines

1. We've seen from our study that wrong anger usually is caused by our desire to control or have power. We *want something,* and the threat of losing it makes us angry. Below, list four circumstances or people over which you want control. To help, think of situations where you have become angry and then analyze *why* this situation made you angry:

(1) _____

(2) _____

(3) _____

(4) _____

Pick two of the above items and place the people or circumstances you want to control in the white "surrender" flags below. In so doing, you are telling the Lord that you recognize you've been trying to exert control where you have no right. Ask for his forgiveness. Tell a close friend what you've done and ask him or her to help you keep them surrendered.

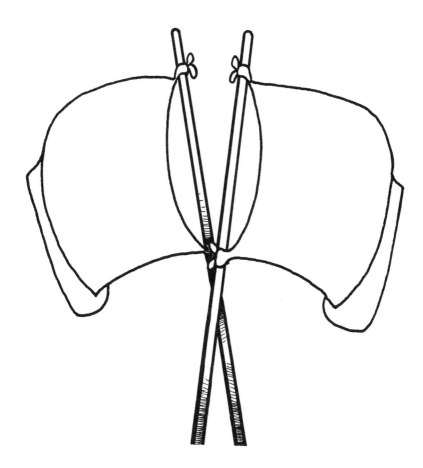

2. You've also learned that "a quick-tempered man does foolish things," and "anger is cruel and fury overwhelming" (Proverbs 14:17; 27:4). Are there any people you've really wounded (emotionally, or maybe even physically) in your anger (a parent, friend, teacher, or co-worker)? Would you be willing to tell them you are trying to deal with your anger and ask them to forgive you for what you said or did? (*Note*: When you ask their forgiveness, be sure to specify what you said or did that hurt them.) You'll never really begin to deal with your anger until you face those who have tasted it the most.

3. Perhaps you have found yourself getting into trouble lately and you can trace it to a *friend* who's got a serious problem with anger. Proverbs 22:24 says, "Do not make friends with a hot-tempered man, do not associate with one easily angered."

Maybe you need to sit down with this friend and share your concern over his or her anger and how it is affecting you and the friendship. If you do, be sure to:

- tell them you value the friendship;

- tell them you're concerned, for their *sake,* about their anger;

- tell them you are concerned about the effect their anger is having on *you,* but you are willing to help;

- tell them you want to try to keep the friendship, but that you'll have to break it off if things don't change.

(*Hint*: Don't be afraid that they'll get mad at you!)

Closing Lines

Stephen and I walked and talked for nearly an hour that day. It was the day I finally felt led to tell him the truth about his anger. We discussed his problem with needing to control others — his obsession with power. Stephen was a trained martial artist, deeply involved in "Dungeons and Dragons" (a power-based fantasy game). He was also seriously studying terrorism and Ninjitsu, the art of the assassin! Slowly he agreed with all of my assessments. He realized that his relationships with girls crumbled because he smothered them with possessiveness or intimidated them with his jealousy, both of which were power moves on his part.

I also told Stephen the even harsher truth that a life of demanding power had nothing to do with knowing, loving, and serving Jesus Christ. A person cannot serve if he has to be in control. He started to see the seriousness of our conversation. We weren't merely discussing the proper way to treat girls; we were beaming a bright light on the darkest shadows of his whole life!

Stephen *knew* that our talk was crucial. He also knew it was true. Unfortunately, Stephen decided after a week or two that the Christian life "wasn't for him." He gravitated to a new girlfriend he could control, and graduation day came. If Stephen doesn't eventually surrender himself to God, his anger will one day consume him and anyone close by.

Anger that seeks to control through power, jealousy, or position is wrong. It's wrong because what it produces has nothing to do with the righteous (Christlike) person God wants us each to become.

Stay away from this unrighteous anger! It shows no mercy and leaves no survivors.

Lifeline

Unrighteous anger comes from my desire to control.

His Lines

Proverbs 22:24-25

James 1:19-20

The Bottom Line
(For Group or One-on-one Discussion)

1. Ask group members to share their thoughts and conclusions about the desire to control being a major cause of unrighteous anger. Have them give examples from their own lives, if they are willing.

2. Have group members discuss TV programs or movies they have recently seen that either soften the seriousness of unrighteous anger or show the reality of its outcome. Have members clip newspaper articles that deal with unrighteous anger being acted out.

3. How can group members creatively help one another deal with unrighteous anger?

4. Ask group members if they want to share their struggles with anger and have the group pray for them. (*Note*: You will need to be careful in how this is handled. Privacy and discretion are essential. But, it can be a very meaningful time.)

5. How do you handle the unrighteous anger of a *parent* toward you? How should you?

3

Being "Good and Mad" Can Be Good

Opening Lines

Sometime during your childhood you probably tuned into "The Dukes of Hazzard" for Friday evening entertainment. It was a predictable plot — bad guys versus good guys, with the bad side winning up to the very last second. High speed car stunts, chases, and wrecks were weekly fare for the orange Dodge Charger christened "The General Lee," before good finally triumphed.

One pudgy man played the key role in the portrayal of all that was wicked, mean, and nasty. His villainous name was "Boss Hogg." He made you mad every week! He owned most of the businesses in Hazzard, held most of the home mortgages, and had his own bank to manage all the money. He even controlled the town's corrupt police force.

Boss Hogg was bad in the truest sense of the word. Well, believe it or not, there's a historical Boss Hogg in the Bible. He lived during the days of Jesus. Although his name appears only three times in the New Testament, a lot can be learned from other historical sources about this first century power broker.

The most influential man in the days when Jesus walked the earth was the Jewish high priest. He held immense social, political, and spiritual authority. The social, legal, and religious systems were one and the same for the Jews. "Separation of church and state" was unheard of. Consequently, whoever exerted power in one sphere controlled them all. Allow me to introduce Annas.

After Annas had been high priest himself, he conveniently saw to it that his sons were appointed to that position so that the role (and power) remained in the family.

The primary money-making scheme for Annas was his operation in the Court of the Gentiles, just outside the temple in Jerusalem. All Jews were required by law to come to Jerusalem annually to fulfill religious duties such as offering sacrifices and paying taxes. But the animals for sacrifice had to be inspected for imperfections; the required temple tax had to be paid in shekels, the currency of Jerusalem; and an offering had to be presented, no matter how poor an individual was.

A person could get currency changed to shekels — for a fee. A person could buy animals for sacrifice — for a fee. A person could have his animal inspected — for a fee. And if someone brought an animal from home which was found to be imperfect, one of the court's perfect sacrifices was graciously offered as a trade-in! For a slight fee, of course. Annas had built an enterprising business out of these religious requirements. Residents of Jerusalem rightly called it "Annas's Bazaar."

Are you beginning to get the picture of this biblical "Boss Hogg." If you were Jesus, and you knew all this was going on around your Father's house, what would *you* do? Would you be angry? And if you were angry, would it be wrong?

On the Lines

1. Let's examine the story of "Jesus' Day at the Bazaar." Actually, Jesus had two "run-ins" with Annas's Bazaar — once in the beginning of his ministry and a second time about three years later, just before he was crucified. Let's look at his first encounter. It's recorded for us in John 2:13-16.

• What was going on in the Temple courts? (verses 13-14)

_____

_____

• What did Jesus *do*? (verse 15)

_____

_____

• What did Jesus *say*? (verse 16)

_____

• Does Jesus seem mildly upset or genuinely angry? Explain.

_____

_____

2. From this first account, it seems like Jesus was angry simply because they were *selling* things. Yet, we know that it would have been a helpful service to the visiting Jews who had traveled hundreds of miles. We can get a bigger picture of *why* Jesus was so angry when we examine his conduct the second time he confronts Annas's Bazaar in Mark 11:15-18.

• Does Jesus seem angry here? (verses 15-16) ☐ yes   ☐ no

• What reason does Jesus give *here* for his actions that sheds more light on why he did what he did? (verse 17)

_____

_____

3. Another example of this type of anger is found in the book of Nehemiah. Read Nehemiah 5:1-5 and summarize what the problem at hand appears to be:

_____

_____

What is Nehemiah's response in 5:6?

_____

4. Can you see what these two examples of anger have in common? In other words, what *brought on* the anger in both cases? Check the box below that you think is the *cause* of the anger:

☐ The person who got angry had been hurt by others' sin.

☐ A religious leader had sinned.

☐ One person's sin had affected innocent people.

5. Look at Ephesians 4:26. From this verse, is it possible to be angry and yet *not* sin? Explain.

_____

_____

_____

What does this verse say to *do* when you are angry?

_____

_____

_____

6. Summarize, from your study, what you think all the verses we've looked at are teaching about when anger is okay, even appropriate.

_____

_____

_____

_____

Between the Lines

1. Can you think of any situations in your life right now where you are the source of unjust pain or hurt in the lives of others (e.g., gossip, selling something for more than it's worth, lying)? What steps would you be willing to take to stop what you're doing or make up for what you've done?

2. Are there any sources of injustice or hurt that *you* could express proper anger toward, or help those who have been hurt by them (e.g., pornography, abortion, rape, homelessness, orphans, widows)? An excellent source of what can be done about injustice is the magazine, *Focus on the Family CITIZEN*. A sample copy can be obtained by writing:

> Focus on the Family Citizen Magazine
> Pomona, CA 91799

(*Note*: If you decide to *do* something based on righteous anger, be careful to differentiate between being angry, and being belligerent or offensive. The two should not be confused.)

Closing Lines

Well, by now you've come to realize that Jesus was "good and mad" over what was happening in Jerusalem . . . but the emphasis must be on the word good. His anger was not *un*righteous anger. And it wasn't okay just because he was God's Son. There *really* is such a thing as *righteous* anger for you and me.

Anger that is the result of the effects of people's sins *on others* is righteous anger. Remember, however, that the people we read about in the Bible were not responding to their *own* hurt. We learned in the last chapter that unrighteous anger comes from my desire to control. Righteous anger is the product of my concern for the impact of sin on *others*.

You'll notice in the biblical accounts that Jesus never hurt or even touched *people*. He spoke the truth to them, but the "whip of cords" he made that day was never used on them. Righteous anger is careful, controlled, and constructive. Unrighteous anger is thoughtless, chaotic, and destructive. One is concerned for *others,* the other is focused on *self.* Be careful, be cautious, but don't be afraid to be angry — as long as it's righteous.

Lifeline

Righteous anger is concerned about sin's effect on *others.*

His Lines

Ephesians 4:26

Mark 3:5

The Bottom Line
(For Group or One-on-one Discussion)

1. When is it appropriate to fight for the rights of the oppressed?

2. "Operation Rescue" is a movement that advocates civil disobedience[1] to discourage doctors from performing abortions. Many people are arrested in the process. Do you think this approach is a legitimate form of righteous anger? Explain.

3. What steps can your group take to become involved in legitimate righteous anger causes? Have someone in the group research the groups/organizations already operating in your city that are dedicated to helping those affected by the sins of others.

4. Is it possible for Christians to become involved in righteous anger causes in which non-Christian (even anti-Christian) groups are involved? Defend your answer.

5. Is it possible for Christians to become so consumed with righteous causes that they neglect or even forget the Christian's primary responsibility of enlarging the kingdom of God? Explain.

---

[1] Civil disobedience is the belief that allegiance to a "higher law" makes breaking a human law permissible, in some cases even necessary.

4

I Don't Get Mad—
I Get Even!

Opening Lines

Diane had been avoiding me for two solid weeks by dodging behind her friends when I walked by, or striking up a quick conversation with someone if she thought I was going to speak to her. We had been friends for several years, partly through her older sister who had been one of our baby-sitters.

Whenever a student went into this "strategic avoidance maneuver," it usually meant one of two things: either I had offended or hurt them in some way, or they were deeply involved in some sin. Either way, I made it a policy to sit down and talk with them if they didn't make some move to seek me out first.

Trying to talk to Diane was like trying to track the Stealth! Finally, one day I spotted her walking ahead of me, alone. I picked up my pace and drew alongside her. "Hi, Diane," I said. A nervous "hello" came out in response. "Don't you think it's about time we talked?" I asked. Diane stopped, stared at the floor, then looked up, her soft eyes filled with tears. She said quietly, "Yeah, I really need to." We made an appointment for lunch that day.

When my fourth hour class ended, I wondered whether or not she would show up. But as I was getting my things together, I looked up and saw her standing in my doorway, lunch in hand. I snatched up my sandwich and we headed for my "office," a large black couch outside the administrative offices.

We wandered around a number of safe topics and eventually realized that we had run out of small talk. "What's going on, Diane?" I probed. The tears began to tumble. "Oh, Mr. Sciacca, I'm not sure I can tell you . . . you'll hate me!" My students all knew that I loved them and believed in them. When they fell, I was there to help them get back up, but they also knew I was saddened when they gave in to sin. So, Diane's comment alerted me to the possibility that she had become involved in something pretty serious, probably sex. I was right.

She proceeded to pour out one of the saddest stories I had heard in a long time. Diane had deliberately surrendered her virginity to a guy she didn't love, had never dated, and hardly even knew! In fact, it was her sister's best friend, who had "dropped by" the house, knowing full well that her parents were out of town.

I was pretty broken by the news. Because my own life in high school had been such a mess, what some of my students *did* didn't shock me, but often *who* did particular things hit me pretty hard. This was one of those times. I wouldn't have guessed Diane would have slept with someone, especially a guy she hardly knew!

What could cause someone like Diane to take such a point-less and damaging step? It was almost as if she were trying to announce something by her act rather than simply seeking pleasure. What was her point?

On the Lines

1. Is sin a static thing? In other words, is it just an act we start and stop, or does sin grow and progress? Look up James 1:13-15. Write out in your own words what you think this verse is saying about whether or not sin is static or progressive.

---

2. Look at Ephesians 4:26, especially the second half of the verse. First of all, what does the phrase, "Do not let the sun go down while you are still angry" mean?

_____

_____

What do you think this verse is telling us to do?

_____

_____

3. Now look at what you put for question 1 above and use it to explain *why* we should deal with our anger, and what might happen if we *don't*.

_____

_____

_____

4. Read Romans 12:17-21. This passage speaks very clearly about one of the things unresolved anger leads to (see verse 19). What is it?

☐ sorrow   ☐ revenge   ☐ bitterness

Why *shouldn't* we take revenge, according to this passage?

_____

_____

5. What *should* be our attitude towards those we are angry with? (Leviticus 19:18)

_____

_____

6. In order to deal with our anger, to keep it from growing, we need to talk to *somebody* about our feelings. Who is the first "somebody" we should talk to? (Psalm 62:8)

_____

_____

7. Write in your own words what the following verses have to say about anger, revenge, and prayer. (You'll have to do some serious thinking here, but that's good!)

Matthew 26:36-50

_____

_____

1 Timothy 2:8

_____

_____

2 Chronicles 16:10

_____

_____

8. Write a brief summary of what you feel is the most important thing you've learned from this chapter about anger, revenge, and God.

_____

_____

_____

_____

Between the Lines

1. Take some time in a quiet place to think: Are there any people toward whom you *are* holding back anger? Have you tried to justify your feelings — or perhaps just ignore them? Write their names (or initials) in the spaces below.

_____

_____

_____

2. Christian psychologist Dr. Archibald Hart has said:

> God knows that our natural tendency is to seek revenge. He also knows that the chain of revenge never ends. If I take out your eye, then you will want to take out mine; I will then want your other eye, and you will retaliate with my second. The result: we will both be blind, and neither will be satisfied. *The cycle of revenge never ends.* This is why anger must be cut off *before* it resorts to revenge.
>
> In Matthew 5:38-48, Jesus is saying to us that the best way to deal with our hurts is to love the ones who are doing the hurting. He calls them our "enemies." The call is for us to exercise forgiveness as the antidote for the anger at being hurt. "Cheek turning" is an act of forgiveness.[2]

But *why* must you give up your desire for revenge (especially if you haven't acted it out) in order to deal with your anger? The answer to that question is found in two verses of Scripture, Micah 7:18 and Ephesians 4:32. Look them up and read them slowly (in the order they are listed). Then look at the names you wrote down above. Write out:

WHAT I *SHOULD* DO ABOUT MY ANGER

_____

_____

_____

[2] Dr. Archibald D. Hart, *The Hidden Link Between Adrenalin & Stress*, (Waco, Tex.: Word Books, 1986), 218.

WHY I SHOULD DO IT

_____

_____

WHAT I *PLAN* TO DO

_____

_____

Closing Lines

I asked Diane that day why she chose to do what she did. Her response shocked me. She said, "I was trying to hurt my father in a way that no one else could." Diane had slept with a near stranger and violated her moral standards to *hurt her father*?! I kept asking questions to fish the rest of the story out of this relational swamp. I discovered that her dad, a prominent insurance broker, was genuinely neglecting her. In fact, he had missed her gymnastic tournament three years in a row to attend a convention in Dallas. He dismissed her tears with the heartless comment, "Honey, it's my *job*!"

Following its normal progression, Diane's hurt became anger and her anger grew until she demanded "payment" — she wanted revenge. The tragedy greater than her father's neglect was the fact that Diane's revenge actually hurt *her* more than him! As is always the case, unresolved anger eats away at those who embrace it. Diane was a wounded soldier, shot by her own gun.

Obviously, Diane could have talked to her father and shared her hurt with him, which is *always* the best first step. But she had already done that, and he just shook it off. What then? There are only two options at this point: get angry and try to get even, or give up the anger to God. Based on what you've learned from the Bible and seen in Diane's life, which do you think is the best choice?

Lifeline

Unresolved anger leads to a desire for revenge.

His Lines

Ephesians 4:32

Micah 7:18

The Bottom Line
(For Group or One-on-one Discussion)

1. Have group members share their summaries from the "On the Lines" section (question 8) and discuss each others' conclusions.

2. Read the quote from Dr. Hart (page 37) aloud. Ask for feedback.

3. Is it true that the person who is angry suffers more than the one toward whom he or she is angry? Explain.

4. Should Christians go to court to sue one another? (See 1 Corinthians 6:1-11 for help.)

5. About five hundred years before Christ, a man named Heraclitus said: "It is difficult to fight against anger; for a man will buy revenge with his soul."[3] What is he saying here? Do you agree? Explain.

---

[3] Heraclitus, quoted in Aristotle's *Politics,* 5.11.

5

What Do You Say to an Angry Mob?

Opening Lines

I detest fire drills. For a teacher, they're sort of like a shoestring breaking when you're trying to sprint. Students file out from the building, stand outside, and socialize as though it were a free period, and then finally shuffle slowly back to their seats. It's impossible to restore interest in the subject again. Classroom routine is finished for the day and, as most of you know, teachers don't always function when routine is disrupted.

The events surrounding the death and resurrection of Jesus Christ was a lot like a fire drill for the leaders in Jerusalem. The Jews relished routine, too. They had a religious calendar marked by specific religious holidays and feasts during which specific things happened at specific times. It was a constant, predictable, cozy system in which everyone played a specific part. Of particular importance was the Jewish temple. The religious life of every Jew revolved around it. The temple was the hub of their faith.

So, when a carpenter named Jesus of Nazareth appeared on the scene and started preaching that *where* they worshiped wasn't as important as *who,* and that the sacrifice God wanted was their hearts more than their sheep — well, things started to get stirred up, to say the least (see John 4:19-24; Matthew 5-7). The comforts of routine were really threatened. Jesus had pulled a *fire drill* on the teachers of his day!

The religious leaders were furious. They decided that this disturbance had to be eliminated. So, Jesus was crucified. But he dealt them another surprise — he rose from the dead! And then his disciples began to preach to the Jews the same message — faith in Jesus Christ, rather than works and religious routine, was necessary to please God. This enraged the religious leaders even more. Any disciple who dared to preach about forgiveness through Jesus Christ became a target. The wrath of the Jewish authorities was upon him.

Stephen was just such a man. The Bible tells us he preached the gospel bravely in the face of tremendous hostility (Acts 6:8-8:1). How did Stephen handle the anger of those who hated Jesus? What did he do? What *didn't* he do? It's one thing to learn how to handle our *own* anger, but what do we do when facing the anger of others?

On the Lines

The entire story of Stephen can be found in Acts chapter 6 through the second verse of chapter 8. For this study, we will first examine Stephen's response to the anger of others. Then we will look at other Scriptures that can help *us* deal with the anger of others.

1. Here are four factors that play a significant role in helping us handle the anger of others:

- How I look (facial expressions, etc.)

- How I speak (tone of voice, etc.)

- What I say or don't say

- My whole perspective (how I see or perceive what's happening)

Below are four passages of Scripture (the first two from the story of Stephen) that deal with the anger of others. After each passage, write in one of the above factors that you believe the Scripture addresses. Then in the spaces provided, write out what you think the Scripture is saying, and how or why you think this would be important in dealing with the anger of others.

Acts 6:12-15

_____

WHAT THE PASSAGE IS SAYING:

_____

WHY THIS IS IMPORTANT:

_____

_____

_____

_____

Acts 7:54-60

_____

WHAT THE PASSAGE IS SAYING:

_____

WHY THIS IS IMPORTANT:

_____

_____

_____

_____

Proverbs 15:1

_____

WHAT THE PASSAGE IS SAYING:

_____

_____

WHY THIS IS IMPORTANT:

_____

_____

_____

_____

Proverbs 20:3

_____

WHAT THE PASSAGE IS SAYING:

_____

_____

WHY THIS IS IMPORTANT:

_____

_____

_____

_____

2. Below are some other verses that discuss how to handle the anger of others. Look them up and write out any thoughts you may have about handling others' anger:

Proverbs 19:19

_____

_____

Proverbs 26:17

_____

_____

Proverbs 26:20

_____

3. Look at your work from questions 1 and 2 above. Below, write out the most important thing you've discovered and *why* it is important to you.

_____

_____

_____

_____

Between the Lines

1. Look back at the four factors from question 1 of "On the Lines." Pick one of the four that you feel is an area where you could improve the way you handle the anger of others (parents, friends, teachers, etc.). Use the suggestions under that category as a guide for constructive changes.

PRINCIPLES	SUGGESTIONS
How I look to those who are angry.	
• Do you roll your eyes, fold your arms, or sigh deeply?	• Seek to relax.
• Do you stare off, or walk away from angry people?	• Make eye contact as much as possible.
• Do you slouch in their presence?	• Don't judge their anger by your facial expressions or body language.
• Are you tense and rigid, especially in your face?	• Listen and ask genuine questions.
How I talk to those who are angry.	
• Do you raise your voice?	• Try not to raise your voice.
• Do you interrupt them while they're speaking?	• Only ask genuine questions, not those intended to make a point — your point.
• Do you talk sarcastically?	• Speak sincerely and warmly.
	• Avoid making lots of "you" statements (i.e., statements that attack and blame).
What I say to those who are angry.	
• Do you speak up when it's none of your business?	• Don't talk a lot. Discipline yourself to listen.
• Do you try to make a point more often than you try to understand?	• Ask questions designed to understand why they're angry.
• Do you talk more than you listen?	• Don't get involved in a quarrel that's not yours to begin with — this includes listening to gossip.
• Are you more concerned about defending yourself than understanding the other person's feelings?	

PRINCIPLES	SUGGESTIONS
How I view the anger of others.	
• Do you see the *person* more than the issue?	• Spend as much time as possible praying for the angry person, even while you are talking to him or her.
• Do you think God has lost control of the situation?	• Spend time reading over the story of Stephen.
• Do you see yourself totally as a victim?	• Ask yourself if the person is angry with you because of something you've done or what you stand for. (If someone is angry with you because you're against things like drinking or premarital sex, or because you won't give them your homework, their anger is not your responsibility and may be beyond your help to begin with.)
• Do you believe you have to change the person's mind?	

Closing Lines

Stephen faced the wrath of the Jewish leaders with quiet courage. Their anger was clearly a result of what Stephen had said, not *how* he had said it. His "body language" was good, and he remained calm and relatively quiet. Stephen's accusers killed him on that day. The sad and sobering truth is that sometimes the anger of others will cause severe pain and possibly death. But that's not the point of this story for us.

Stephen stands as an excellent example of how to face the anger of others. In fact, Stephen patterned *his* response after Jesus himself. Jesus confronted the anger of others with a calm and quiet confidence.

You and I will face the anger of others frequently in our lifetime. It may come from within our own homes. Although we may not be able to control whether or not the anger exists, how we respond to that anger *can* have a significant impact on what the anger *becomes*. How we talk, how we look, and what we think and say (or don't say) are important factors in dealing with the anger of others. Although we may not be able to *change* others, we can *affect* them.

So, what *do* you say to an angry mob? Maybe nothing!

Lifeline

My reactions to angry people can affect what their anger becomes.

His Lines

Proverbs 15:1

1 Peter 2:23

The Bottom Line
(For Group or One-on-one Discussion)

1. What should a Christian do when confronted by an angry person who could become physically abusive or violent?

2. What responsibility do we have, if any, to protect the "weak" from angry people? What form should that protection take?

3. If a friend who has a genuine problem with anger expresses a desire for help, what should you do?

4. Have group members share their answers to question 3 of "On the Lines." Discuss the various responses and why they differed.

5. Have group members share some defeats and victories in dealing with the anger of others (e.g., home, school, etc.).

6

Holy Smoke

Opening Lines

A man by the name of H. L. Mencken made the following statement about God:

> I see little evidence in this world of the so-called goodness of God. On the contrary, it seems to me that, on the strengths of his daily acts, He must be set down a most stupid, cruel and villainous fellow.[4]

A cold shiver ascends my spine as I contemplate Mencken's gross misrepresentation of God. I wonder how anyone would dare speak of our Lord like this! But before I cast too severe a judgment upon Mr. Mencken, I am reminded of something I brashly concluded about God over twenty years ago, before I became a Christian:

> You know nothing of the world in which you live, let alone those beyond!! You kill to survive and then will destroy yourself. If we *were* made in the image and likeness of God, then I sadly say that I think less of him than I do his worthless creations.

---

[4]H.L. Mencken, quoted in Burton Stevenson, *The Home Book of Quotations, Classical and Modern* (New York: Greenwich House, 1984), 798.

I believe that Mencken and I both arrived at this terribly mistaken view of God by assuming that God was very much like what he had made. In other words, because Mr. Mencken and I saw so much cruelty and stupidity in other people, we assumed God was like that too. Whenever anyone ascribes human characteristics to God, or seeks to understand God's qualities in terms of human behavior, that person arrives at a mental image of God that's more human than divine, more like himself than God. And that's very inaccurate.

This becomes extremely important when reading the Bible, our primary source of information about God. If, when I read in Scripture that God gets angry, I think in terms of human anger, then God seems petty, immature, and unpredictable (see Numbers 32:10-12 as an example of when God became angry).

If, on the other hand, I realize that God is holy (set apart from everything else) and perfect, then his anger takes on a totally different meaning. It becomes holy and perfect anger, something you and I cannot comprehend, much less express.

Since God's anger is holy anger, it can't be saturated with the selfish sin that characterizes most human anger. His is proper and deserved anger. But what *makes* God angry in the first place? Are there actually certain behaviors and attitudes that arouse the anger of God? If so, what are they?

On the Lines

1. Before we explore what actually angers God, let's examine some basic truths about the nature of his anger Look up the verses below and write out your answers to these questions:

- what the verse is saying about God's anger;

- why it is important;

- what it tells me about God's character.

Exodus 34:6

WHAT IT SAYS ABOUT GOD'S ANGER

WHY IT IS IMPORTANT

_____

_____

_____

WHAT IT TELLS ME ABOUT GOD'S CHARACTER

_____

_____

_____

Psalm 30:5

WHAT IT SAYS ABOUT GOD'S ANGER

_____

_____

_____

WHY IT IS IMPORTANT

_____

_____

WHAT IT TELLS ME ABOUT GOD'S CHARACTER

_____

_____

_____

2. Let's look at some of the things that make God angry. Below is a list of verses that speak of things that anger God or things he hates. Read the verse on the left a few times and then match it with the word or phrase on the right that best fits:

_____ Numbers 11:1	A. worshiping other "gods"
_____ Psalm 78:13-22	B. causing conflict among friends
_____ 2 Kings 22:17	C. unbelief
_____ Romans 1:18	D. suppressing the truth
_____ 1 Thessalonians 2:16	E. lying about others
_____ Proverbs 6:16, 19a	F. complaining
_____ Proverbs 6:16, 19b	G. suppressing the preaching of the gospel

3. There's one final truth about God's anger and you (if you are a Christian) that we need to look at. What do Romans 5:9-11 and 1 Thessalonians 1:10 teach about the anger of God and the Christian? Check the box with the correct answer.

☐ God no longer is angered over the things that made him angry in the Old Testament. He has changed his mind over what makes him angry.

☐ God's anger has not changed. It was poured out on Jesus on the cross so that I wouldn't have to experience it. But that *doesn't* mean God has changed his mind about the things that make him angry.

☐ God no longer *gets* angry because all his anger was poured out on Jesus. He has no anger left.

Between the Lines

1. Go back to your answers to question 2 in "On the Lines." Pick two of the eight things that anger God that are in *your* life. Be honest! Write out below how you feel they *show up* in your life and *why* you think they anger God. Think carefully. Be thorough.

ITEM #1

_____

_____

_____

_____

_____

ITEM #2

_____

_____

_____

_____

_____

2. Ask yourself the following questions:

Do you excuse these behaviors in your life because they don't seem like such a big deal compared to others' sins?

☐ yes ☐ no

Do you justify your anger by telling yourself God will forgive you (or already has) if you do them?

☐ yes ☐ no

Do you believe that God is so upset with you that you're beyond help or beyond hope?

☐ yes   ☐ no

3. If you answered "yes" to either of the first two questions above, you need to be reminded that the punishment Jesus endured was *because of these sins.* But just because he "took the rap" for you does not mean that what made God angry in the first place is any less serious now.

Remember, it was a violation of God's holiness that caused his anger in the first place. And that hasn't changed at all. Maybe you need to spend some time right now and tell God you've been focusing so much on Jesus' death for you, that you've neglected to think about what *caused* that death. You also need to take some steps to stop these behaviors. Who can you talk to who will help hold you accountable to stop? Call him or her today and ask for help.

If you answered "yes" to the third question in number 2 above, you probably are focusing too much on God's anger and neglecting the fact that Jesus Christ *bore that anger for you.* Regardless of your sin, God's anger toward you has been completely absorbed. You need to focus on the forgiveness that is yours through Jesus Christ. God is not mad at you. Memorize Isaiah 1:18. Dwelling on God's holy anger without balancing it with his holy forgiveness will lead you to be legalistic.

Closing Lines

Images of an angry God, out of control, blowing smoke and spitting fire *are* primitive and unbalanced. But the idea of a God who winks at sin and says, "that's cool — I understand" is equally false. God's anger is the result of his holiness, not his immaturity. Because he is eternal and unchanging, what angers him never changes.

That means, as a Christian, I should seek that which pleases him and avoid that which doesn't, *even though* I'm forgiven. In fact, I should do it especially *because* I'm forgiven.

Holy smoke precedes holy fire. Just because I will be spared the fire doesn't mean I shouldn't heed the smoke!

Lifeline

The things that anger God should not be a part of my life.

His Lines

Exodus 34:6

Romans 1:18

The Bottom Line
(For Group or One-on-one Discussion)

1. How can a Christian have a proper and healthy balance between understanding God's holiness (i.e., anger) and his love (i.e., forgiveness)?

2. Some say, "How could a loving God send anyone to hell?" What's wrong with that question, based on your study from this chapter?

3. Is the idea of a wrathful, angry God really primitive? Explain.

4. Should the things that make God angry make me angry too? Explain. If so, what should I do (if anything) about them?

5. Idolatry was one of the things that angered God. What are our idols today? (An idol is anything I give my greatest devotion to.) What can we do about these idols?